OLD AGE
FOR
Beginners

Clive Whichelow

ILLUSTRATIONS BY IAN BAKER

summersdale

OLD AGE FOR BEGINNERS

An Hachette UK Company
www.hachette.co.uk

Summersdale Publishers Ltd
Part of Octopus Publishing Group Limited
Carmelite House
50 Victoria Embankment
LONDON
EC4Y 0DZ
UK

www.summersdale.com

Printed and bound in China

ISBN: 978-1-78783-681-5

Substantial discounts on bulk quantities of Summersdale books are available to corporations, professional associations and other organizations. For details contact general enquiries: telephone: +44 (0) 1243 771107 or email: enquiries@summersdale.com.

INTRODUCTION

Well, you're not exactly a beginner, are you? In fact, you've been working on this for some time. You stretched middle age out as far as it could possibly go, all the while pretending that it was in fact an extended youth, then you had to admit defeat, give in and start acting like a PMP (Proper Middle-aged Person).

You got used to wearing clothes that were more comfortable than fashionable, having opinions that would raise the hackles of anyone under 30 and learning to love your laughter lines, but now it's time to become a POP (Proper Older Person), and you know what, it's going to be a lot of fun!

Have you noticed how older people can say the most outrageous things and get away with it? Any younger, and you'd have the thought police knocking on your door and hauling you off to some tribunal, but once you're over a certain age people tend to indulge you a bit more. "Eccentric" covers a multitude of sins.

You'll also be able to dress however you damn well please, because you're not a fashion victim any more. Grey hair is a great blank canvas on which to experiment with colour, and the wrinkles will add a bit of personality to your tattoos!

You may just find that being older is the best time of your life, but don't tell younger people that or they'll all be jumping on the bandwagon.

WHAT IS OLD AGE?

It's what comes between
middle age and dotage

It's when all those charities
start giving back to you!

It's when you realize that 60
wasn't really that old

It's when lying about your age
involves taking 30 years off

WHAT DO I HAVE TO DO IN OLD AGE?

It's time to finally get around to all those things you've been meaning to do – you've got no excuses now!

Have fun! Most of the things you spent your life worrying about never happened, did they?

Stop trying to be a role model for younger people – leave that to the pop stars and football players

THINGS YOU SHOULDN'T BE DOING NOW

Trying to keep up with the latest street slang – what's wrong with "fab", "hip" and "groovy"? They might even come back into fashion

Worrying about your weight – that's why they invented "comfort fit"

Caring what anyone else thinks – what do they know anyway?

Holding in your stomach on the beach – as you used to say once, "Let it all hang out!"

HOW YOU IMAGINED OLD AGE VERSUS THE REALITY

IMAGINED	REALITY
Giving your long-acquired pearls of wisdom to younger members of the family	Giving large chunks of your long-acquired cash to younger members of your family
Going on exotic cruises with your hard-earned pension	Making exotic curses about your hard-up pension
Writing your fascinating memoirs about a long and colourful life	Trying to remember what you did yesterday

ODD THINGS THAT MIGHT HAPPEN NOW

DIY will become SEDIFY
(Someone Else Does It For You)

On TV quiz shows you have no knowledge
of the pop music of the past 40 years

After your long, slow shift from
rock to easy listening, you are now
seriously considering making a
permanent switch to classical

You find you have more
pairs of slippers than shoes

WIT AND WISDOM
YOU WILL ACQUIRE

If I knew then what I know now I wouldn't have done what I did, so it's lucky I can't remember most of it!

It's hardly worth going on a diet now, is it?

Anyone can be young, but being old takes years of experience

WAYS IN WHICH TO SMOOTH THE TRANSITION

Get a walking stick – even if you
don't need one – and break it in

Acquire a taste for crooners, brass
bands and Sousa marches

Start using age-appropriate language, e.g.
calling people "sweetie", "young man", etc.

Start watching age-appropriate TV shows – costume dramas, antiques shows and anything that advertises stair-lifts in the break

CONVERSATIONS YOU WILL NO LONGER HAVE

Asking the shop assistant if they do
the jeans in a smaller waist size

Asking the hotel receptionist on holiday
where the nearest nightclubs are

Actually telling people when
it's your birthday

CONVERSATIONS YOU
MIGHT START HAVING

Asking the shop assistant for the size
in feet, as inches sounds too big

Asking the hotel receptionist on
holiday if you can have the room
farthest from the nearest nightclub

Feigning surprise when someone else
mentions it's your birthday – especially
if it's another of those milestone ones

THINGS YOU NO LONGER HAVE TO FEEL GUILTY ABOUT

Taking up a bus or train seat when an old person is standing – they may be younger than you!

Getting younger people to lift heavy things for you – you may even be one of those heavy things yourself!

Listing your dietary requirements before eating at someone else's house – you might even feel quite trendy!

PEOPLE WHO MAY NOW
EYE YOU WITH SUSPICION

Café owners who think you'll make a cup
of tea last all day just to be in the warm

People who accept a lift in your
car and wonder if you can see
beyond the front bumper

Doctors who are expecting you to
reel off a long list of conditions,
illnesses, allergies and complaints that
will run into their lunch break

Gym owners who think
you might keel over at any
moment and jack up their
insurance premium

WHAT OLD AGE SHOULDN'T BE

Dull – you're no longer tied down with mortgages, kids and jobs. Live a little!

Pipe and slippers – this isn't 1954, you know!

Slow – slow, slow, quick, quick, slow maybe…

HOW YOU WILL BE VIEWED BY YOUNGER FRIENDS AND RELATIVES

As someone virtually guaranteed
to say something inappropriate or
politically incorrect at any moment

As someone who probably has a lot of
money stashed away (sadly untrue!)

As someone with amazing survival skills
after a lifetime of drinking, smoking and
making the most of the Swinging Sixties

As someone who lost interest
in fashion circa 1974

THINGS THAT WILL MAKE YOU FEEL NOT AS OLD AS SOME PEOPLE

When you overtake someone else
walking down the street

When you don't yet qualify
for a senior's discount

When you curse an elderly driver
crawling along in front of you

HOW THINGS WILL CHANGE AS YOU GET OLDER

You enjoy the TV reruns more
than the current shows

You notice that everyone seems
to be speaking more quietly

You can watch a TV "celebrity special"
without knowing who any of them are

THINGS YOU CAN DO NOW

Get discounts – even though you might be
better off than a lot of younger people!

Be perfect – you have now learned
from all your mistakes

Enlist younger members of the family
for little jobs around the house, ferrying
you around and generally fetching
and carrying (it's payback time!)

THINGS YOU SHOULDN'T COMPLAIN ABOUT

Milestone birthdays – each one
is now a major achievement

Prices in the shops – you get discounted
travel and special seniors' deals. What
more do you want, free alcohol?

The "younger generation" – let's
face it, pretty much everyone is the
"younger generation" to you now

Noisy neighbours.
If you can hear them then
at least you know your
hearing's still good!

THINGS YOU SHOULD COMPLAIN ABOUT

People who talk about you as if you're not there ("Would they like the soup?")

People who just assume you're not on the internet

The tiny buttons on mobile phones

TRUTHS THAT WILL SLOWLY DAWN ON YOU

Most people will be completely bewildered by your stock of comedy catchphrases and cultural reference points ("Who loves ya, baby?")

You may not become famous after all

Older people live in bungalows for a reason

Police officers don't
just *look* younger

MYSTERIES **OF OLD AGE**

When your stock of memories is
longer than ever before, why can't
you remember anything?

Now you have lots of time to do things,
why is your body refusing to play ball?

Why are you ageing at a different rate
from all the celebrities you grew up with?

FANTASY **INTERLUDE**

An Aldabra giant tortoise lived
to the age of 255, so imagine if
humans lived that long!

At the age of 100 you still
wouldn't be middle-aged

At the age of 50 you would probably
be still living with your parents

People wouldn't think you were
old until you were around 180

NEW DEFINITIONS
YOU MIGHT NEED

Junior doctor – one under 65

Gentle workout – not working out at all

White-knuckle ride – being in a car driven
by someone even older than yourself

THINGS YOU CAN DO NOW THAT YOU COULDN'T BEFORE

Watch an old film without remembering
you've seen it before (at least twice)

Apply for "National Treasure" status

Behave outrageously and be
indulged as "a character"

Plead infirmity whenever
any work needs doing

YOUR NEW
RESPONSIBILITIES

Wondering what the
world is coming to

Fighting a one-person
campaign to stop it

Writing indignant letters
to the newspapers

EXPERT AGEING ADVICE YOU COULD DISH OUT

Age is all in the mind –
like this: 'mAGinEd

You're only as old as you
feel, so don't feel old

If you've got no laughter lines you
haven't had enough laughs

There's always someone older than you – OK, it might be a giant tortoise, but whatever!

TV SHOWS THEY SHOULD HAVE FOR OLDER PEOPLE

The Price Is Right Out of My Budget

Who Wants to Have a Head of Hair?

Short-Sighted Date

Meal or No Meal and Pay the Heating Bill Instead

THINGS YOUNGER PEOPLE WILL SAY TO YOU

What was it like in the olden days?

How did you manage without
a smartphone?

How did you get anywhere
without satnav?

(And whatever they say it will probably be
said very s l o w l y and very LOUDLY)

PURSUITS FOR OLDER PEOPLE

Trying to keep warm rather
than trying to be cool

Spending on a sunny day rather
than saving for a rainy day

Getting up at dawn rather than
getting down till dawn

JUST THINK...

There are almost 16 million people
over 60 in the UK, and 74 million in
the US – that's twice the population of
Argentina! Let's form our own country!

Television would be classic
sitcoms instead of reality TV

People would write proper letters
instead of sending texts

Everyone would speak properly
and have good manners (hey, this
really is fantasy land, isn't it?!)

Pubs and bars would be quiet enough to have a conversation in, and over 60s would get discounted drinks

UPSIDES AND DOWNSIDES OF OLD AGE

The Upside of Old Age …
You have years of experience
… and the Downside
You don't seem to have
learned much from it

The Upside of Old Age …
Memory Lane is getting longer
… and the Downside
The other end of it is
increasingly out of focus

SONGS YOU MIGHT FIND YOURSELF SINGING

"Brown Suede Shoes"

"Hair, There and Everywhere"

"Let's Spend the Night Together
(Ode to a Hot-Water Bottle)"

"Limping Jack Flash"

PEOPLE YOU'LL SEE MORE OF NOW

Your doctor – though with a bit of luck
it will only be on the golf course

Your neighbours – though whether you
consider that a bonus is up for discussion!

Door-to-door salespeople – though you
can have lots of fun pretending to be
senile and wasting hours of their time

BE ORIGINAL

Don't take it easy, take it neat!

Don't *talk* about the "good old days"
– *have* plenty more good old days

Don't moan about new technology
– invent an app to do it for you!

AN OLDER PERSON'S DAY

9.00 a.m. – Wake up and
think about getting up

10.00 a.m. – Get up

10.30 a.m. – A spot of breakfast

11.30 a.m. – A well-earned snooze

12.30 a.m. – A spot of lunch

1.00 p.m. – A well-earned snooze

3.00 p.m. – Flick through the TV channels

6.00 p.m. – Absolutely nothing
on! Crack open a drink

9.00 p.m. – What an exhausting
day! Start getting ready for bed

NEW NAMES FOR YOUR HOUSE

Belly Acres

Blurry View

Restonme Laurels

The Past-Caring Home

OLD AGE DREAMS
VERSUS REALITY

DREAM	REALITY
Finally having the time to make your garden look beautiful	Having to pay someone else to do it because it's too much like hard work
Having a big family gathering for your next milestone birthday	After a couple of glasses of wine you'll probably sleep through most of it
Turning all your old photos into a proper pictorial history of your life	Realizing that the last few years of them are on some electronic device you have no clue how to operate
Tracking down all your long-lost relatives and compiling a definitive family tree	Finding out your extended family is less like the Waltons and more like the Borgias

THINGS YOU CAN BLAME
YOUR AILMENTS ON

Dodgy knees – too much kneeling
in church (obviously!)

Dodgy back – too much bending over
backwards trying to please other people

Dodgy hip – doing The Twist rather too
enthusiastically back in the sixties

Dodgy hearing – turning your
electric guitar amp up to "11"

NAMES YOU MIGHT NOW GET CALLED

Wrinkleton

Coffin-dodger

Silver surfer – even if your internet
activities are limited to finding recipes
and solving household problems

THINGS THAT YOU MIGHT FIND ENCOURAGING

Most of your favourite pop stars
from way back when are still going
strong and you probably didn't
have their drink/drug intake

Lying about your age will only
get easier – the older you get, the
harder it will be to remember

What with new knees, new hips
and all the rest, you could be
virtually bionic one day!

HOW TO REBRAND OLD AGE

A second crack at youth

It's not the years on the clock that
count – it's the gas in the tank

The autumn of your years
with a spring in your step

ALTERNATIVE WAYS
TO KEEP FIT

Sit-ups – but only to the table
for breakfast, lunch, etc.

Weights – hoisting your own weight
around should be quite sufficient

Running – to the bathroom in
the middle of the night

Burpees – usually just
after drinkees

HOW TO TELL IF YOU'RE TOO OLD TO DRIVE

Everything still looks blurry even *after* you've washed the windscreen

People are strangely reluctant to take up your offers of a lift

Getting in and out of the car takes longer than the actual journey

THINGS YOU WON'T BE GOING TO THE DOCTOR WITH NOW

Stress from working too hard

Looking for something to slow you down

Asking for a sick note

Sports injuries

PHONE APPS FOR THE OLDER PERSON

One that reminds you when
to take your pills

One that lets you know when
it's "drink o'clock"

One that can tell you what
you went upstairs for

HOBBIES FOR THE OLDER PERSON

Complaining – about everything, because
nothing is as good as it used to be

Stamp collecting – on your passport as
you're finally free to do what you want

Fishing – for compliments on how
remarkably young you still look

Painting – your spouse knows
you now have no excuse
not to do the decorating

HOW TO INTERPRET THE HEADLINES IN THE PAPER

Holiday Travel Chaos – who cares?
Every day's a holiday for me now

Mortgage Rates to Rise – mortgage?
What mortgage?

Global warming to increase – hooray!
My heating bills cost a fortune these days

HOW WATCHING TV WILL BE DIFFERENT NOW

Breakfast TV's a bit early for you now so you might have to record it

You no longer look at the schedules for ordinary TV, but scour the oldies channels for proper old movies with actors you've actually heard of

Now that you've been around so long and seen everything, even the news seems like repeats now

The volume will have neighbours banging on your wall – luckily, you might not be able to hear it!

THINGS THAT ARE BETTER WHEN YOU'RE OLDER

Nostalgia – you've got more
to be nostalgic about!

Getting cold-callers on the phone
– you've got more time to string
them along and waste their time

Fancy-dress parties – you can look twenty
years younger without cosmetic surgery

PERFECT PART-TIME JOBS FOR THE OLDER GENERATION

Artist's model – you sit for hours without moving anyway, so why not be paid for it?

Tour guide – you have by now probably visited every monument and tourist attraction there is and won't need much training

Consumer rights consultant – after a lifetime of complaining to various utility companies, you are now an expert whose advice will be extremely valuable

Shock jock – your politically incorrect views will boost the radio station's listening figures

PURSUITS THAT SUDDENLY SEEM DANGEROUS

Putting your socks on standing
up – all that balancing on one leg
isn't as easy as it used to be

Making a cup of tea – holding the
kettle at arm's length so you can
see it properly makes pouring the
water out fraught with danger

Using a satnav in the car – mishearing
"slow, speed limit for three miles" as
"no speed limit for three miles" could
lead to a complicated insurance claim

AND THE GOOD NEWS IS...

You have now outlived most of the people
who told you your lifestyle was unhealthy

You can tell all sorts of untruths
about the past because no one else
can remember that far back!

You are now finally a respected pillar
of the community – lucky they
don't know the truth, isn't it?

Anything you do, from opening a tin of sardines to walking around the block, can be seen as a major achievement for someone of your years

If you're interested in finding out more about our books, find us on Facebook at **Summersdale Publishers**, on Twitter at **@Summersdale** and on Instagram at **@summersdalebooks**.

www.summersdale.com